Dogs on Duty

Military Dogs

by Marie Brandle

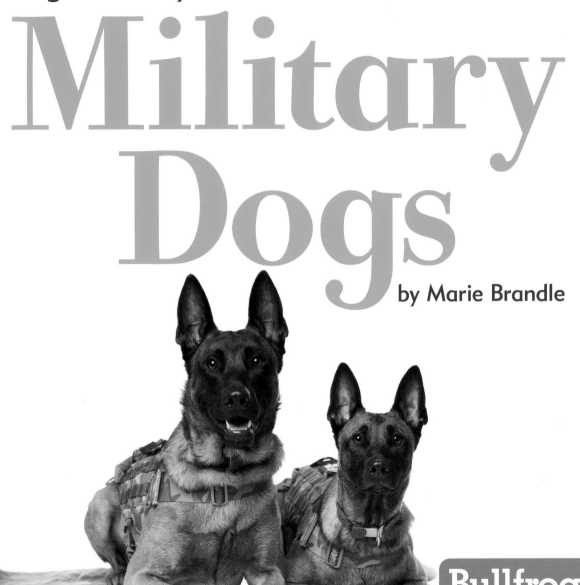

Bullfrog Books

Ideas for Parents and Teachers

Bullfrog Books let children practice reading informational text at the earliest reading levels. Repetition, familiar words, and photo labels support early readers.

Before Reading

- Discuss the cover photo. What does it tell them?

- Look at the picture glossary together. Read and discuss the words.

Read the Book

- "Walk" through the book and look at the photos. Let the child ask questions. Point out the photo labels.

- Read the book to the child, or have him or her read independently.

After Reading

- Prompt the child to think more. Ask: Did you know about military dogs before reading this book? What more would you like to learn about them?

Bullfrog Books are published by Jump!
5357 Penn Avenue South
Minneapolis, MN 55419
www.jumplibrary.com

Library of Congress Cataloging-in-Publication Data

Names: Brandle, Marie, 1989– author.
Title: Military dogs / by Marie Brandle.
Description: Minneapolis, MN: Jump!, Inc., [2022]
Series: Dogs on duty | "Bullfrog books."
Audience: Ages 5–8
Identifiers: LCCN 2021014973 (print)
LCCN 2021014974 (ebook)
ISBN 9781645279280 (hardcover)
ISBN 9781645279297 (paperback)
ISBN 9781645279303 (ebook)
Subjects: LCSH: Dogs—War use
United States—Juvenile literature.
Classification: LCC UH100 .B73 2022 (print)
LCC UH100 (ebook) | DDC 355.4/24—dc23
LC record available at https://lccn.loc.gov/2021014973
LC ebook record available at https://lccn.loc.gov/2021014974

Editor: Eliza Leahy
Designer: Molly Ballanger

Photo Credits: Alexandr Zagibalov/Shutterstock, cover (soldier); U.S. Army, cover (dog), 5, 10–11, 20–21, 23tr, 23br; Erik Lam/Shutterstock, 1; U.S. Air Force, 3, 4, 6–7, 8, 12–13, 18–19, 22tl, 22tr, 22bl, 23tl, 23bl; U.S. Marine Corps, 9, 22br, 24; U.S. Air National Guard, 14–15; AB Forces News Collection/Alamy, 16; Aneta Jungerova/Shutterstock, 17.

Printed in the United States of America at Corporate Graphics in North Mankato, Minnesota.

Table of Contents

Brave Dogs

This dog flies on a plane.

Why?

He is in the military!

He works with soldiers.

5

Each dog has a handler.

Handlers train them.

The dogs learn to listen.

handler

Dogs learn to find bombs.
How?
They sniff for them.

8

They learn to bite
if they need to.

Look out!

9

vest

This dog wears a vest.
It keeps him safe.

This dog wears goggles.
Her ears are covered, too.
Why?

goggles

parachute

She jumps out of a plane.
Cool!

This dog guards a building.

He barks if danger comes.
This warns his handler.

17

This dog searches
a building.

She sniffs for bombs.

These dogs are brave.
They keep soldiers safe!

On the Job

Military dogs have many jobs. Take a look at some of them!

detection dog
This dog searches for drugs by sniffing for them.

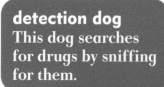

explosives dog
This dog searches for explosives, such as bombs.

patrol dog
This dog patrols, or walks around an area, to find enemies or danger.

sentry dog
This dog guards buildings.

Picture Glossary

handler
A person who trains or controls an animal.

military
The armed forces of a country.

sniff
To smell by taking short breaths in through the nose.

soldiers
People who serve in an army.

Index

To Learn More

Finding more information is as easy as 1, 2, 3.

❶ Go to www.factsurfer.com

❷ Enter "militarydogs" into the search box.

❸ Choose your book to see a list of websites.

24